MARTHA JANSSEN

SECRET SHAME

I Am a Victim of Incest

Augsburg

Minneapolis

Cover design: Lecy Design

Library of Congress Cataloging-in-Publication Data

Janssen, Martha.
   [Silent scream]
   Secret shame / Martha Janssen.
      p. cm.
   Previously published as: Silent scream. c1983.
   ISBN 0-8066-2542-2
   1. Incest victims—Poetry. I. Title.
PS3560.A5356S5   1991
811'.54—dc20   91-4398
                                      CIP

The paper used in this publication meets the minimum requirements
of American National Standard for Information Sciences—Permanence
of Paper for Printed Library Materials, ANSI Z329.48-1984. ∞™

Manufactured in the U.S.A.   AF 9-2542

95   94   93   92   91   1   2   3   4   5   6   7   8   9   10

Contents

A Word to the Reader

I am a victim of incest. My family was middle-class, educated, and respectable. But incest happens often to the girls in our society (and to the boys as well). Father-daughter incest is the most frequently reported form of the abuse and the most likely to do lasting harm to the child. Because it happens in families, it is immensely destructive to a child's sense of trust and it is kept secret because of the threat it poses to family security.

I blamed myself. Children do that, even though the abuse happens because parents do not control themselves and do not honor a child's personal dignity. Because my parents behaved inappropriately, betraying my trust, and because there was no one I could tell, I carried the unspoken burdens of guilt and shame, self-doubt and sadness, fear and anger. My pain became rage, and it was repressed within me—a silent scream, a secret shame.

Telling my feelings to you as I relive them is part of my healing process. It is redemptive to offer my experience to others who suffer, or to those people in homes, schools, clinics, or churches who may better hear, discern, and understand because of this book. Your sensitivity to my experience gives me hope and helps rebuild my trust. To survivors and victims I say: Do not give up hope! Find safe help and tell the truth.

I hope you will understand that I publish this book under a name that is neither my own nor that of my parents or children. That is a matter of protection for myself and my children, for the world has not yet acknowledged or understood the dynamics of this problem. I look for the day when we need not be silent anymore.

MARTHA JANSSEN

PRESCHOOL

Arms

I was small
   and wanted arms
   strong and welcoming
which would open and
encircle me in love.
Hold me
   my small heart
   and tiny body asked.
Hold the child.
Show me love.

Your arms were there
   but stiff.
And when they opened
there were hands
   not to welcome
   but to pry.
Because I could not
trust those hands
I have never known
the love of father's arms.

Bath Time

Bath time was fun!
Warm water
   sometimes bubbly
and a funny shade on my head
to keep shampoo from my eyes
so I wouldn't cry.
Darkness outside
and warm lights in the house.
Usually Mother washed me.
Sometimes Daddy helped.
I didn't know
that he was having "extra" fun.
When he laughed
he laughed with me—
or so I thought
because I was only three.

Then I was thirty, bathing myself.
I realized I seldom washed.
I scrubbed
   scraping away the dirt
   of a confused memory.
Now my tears are not from shampoo.
I weep for the innocent little girl
who couldn't know
the darkness yet to come.

Tears

I was four
(or maybe two).
I cried
because Mother left for a luncheon
and I wanted to go too.
You were there to take care of me.
I cried too long
and you hit me hard.
I never forgot.
I hardly ever cry anymore.

Plea

Why do you hate me, Daddy?
I'm a nice girl.
I behave.
I do what Mommy tells me
and I talk nice to all the grown-ups.
Look, Daddy.
See?
I smile.
I hardly ever cry anymore.
But you want more.
What is it you want?
I'll do anything you say.
I want you to like me.
Please.

Laps

Daughters love to sit
on daddies' laps.
Me too.
I would scramble up
at the end of the day.
We'd talk until Mother left the room.
Then we'd "play."

Now I know
why I watch so carefully
little girls sitting
on their daddies' laps.

Four Years Old

I always sang for company.
You'd play piano
and I'd sing good night
    or dance a bit.
Everybody liked the show.
Even me.

I was used to performing
    for you.

Mysterious Delight

Company came
and I got to stay up late
with the grown-ups
because I was the biggest.
They'd laugh and sing
    play cards and tell jokes
    that I didn't understand.
Everybody said
I was Daddy's little girl.
And I'd smile
as you picked me up
to give me a kiss.
You'd give my bottom
a special pat
as you held me.
Then when I got down
you'd laugh.
It was a special laugh,
as if it contained
years of repressed delight.
I can still hear that laugh.
It scares me.

Charming Child

Funny, but I know
I was a charming child.
It was natural.
Children love learning and life.
People liked me
because I seemed to be
especially delighted by living.
I was.
But somewhere in those days
I also learned
what it means to be not sure
   of people
   of parents
   or the possibility of tomorrow.
The charming child
had a whirlpool inside her
and constantly pulled herself
away from its destruction.
I fought to keep my spirit
alive.

Rules

Lessons.
Little girls sit still
   and don't twirl their skirts
   so much.
Don't tattle.
Talk nice to grown-ups.
Don't talk to strangers—
   they might hurt you.
Mind Mommy
   and Daddy.

Fourth Commandment

They taught me
not to hate my parent.
Families must love each other
no matter what.

From time to time
I did so love the attention—
    your touch
    closeness
    privacy.
Maybe, I thought,
this is what families are for.

It was a sad thing
to discover that those
fleeting tender moments
were not parental loving
but a selfish exploitation
    of parental power.

It is sad
and it comes back to me
again and again.

YOUNG CHILD

Knowledge

Play and pleasure
changed to fear and mistrust
the day that someone said
"That's not the way
parents and children act."
I'd never known that before.
And now I had a terrible secret
which I could never tell—
ever.

Image

It doesn't happen in the
nicer homes.
Respectable people
who go to church
and live in clean neighborhoods
aren't inclined to such
activities.

That's the problem
don't you see.
Not a person I could tell
would want to believe me.
It would ruin the
neighborhood image.

Coaxing

When I'd hesitate
you'd coax me.
Your voice was unusually
   nice
    enticing.
I'd acquiesce
because I didn't know
how to disagree
and I hoped someday
to please you.

Obedience

You insisted.
I crinkled my face
and my lip quivered
but you took my hand
so I followed you
   small steps
   doubling large.
If I drew back
you'd give my arm a jerk
and it was hard to keep my balance
so I followed.
I obeyed.
Children do that, after all.

Danger

Danger threatened!
I knew I had to get away
but there was no place I could go.
A girl of six
can hardly leave
the yard alone.
I stayed.

Instead, I ran into my mind.
I dodged between the messages
of Mother's eyes
and Grandma's sighs—
messages which said
   don't tell the truth
   we cannot bear to hear.

Cowering in the dark recesses
of an attic in my head,
I crept behind the broken furniture
of my unacceptable rage and fear.
Dust of decades,
my forbidden secret,
settled over me as I choked on shame.
Abandoned and abused,
I sealed the doors
so that no one would know.

Protection

Nobody took care of me.
I was seven
and I couldn't run away.
I couldn't tell
nor shield myself.
I was small.
Children need protection.
But nobody knew.
Nobody took care of me.

Mother

Mother loved me.
She told me little girls
should be very good—
but she loved me.
I never told her
I wasn't always good.
He told me I mustn't tell
and she would have cried
or not believed me.
So I never told her.
She wouldn't want to know.
Mother loved me
so I didn't want to hurt
or disappoint her.

Quiet

No one ever heard us
because you'd wait
until the children were asleep
and Mom was gone.
You'd have a place in the house
where we wouldn't be seen
without warning.
There was no reason to yell.
No one would hear.

Alone

A little girl of seven
sits on the front steps
   alone
   pensive.
She carries a burden
so unacceptable and heavy
she cannot let it into
her thoughts
but only feels its weight
inside her
unnamed.

The child is not a child
except in stature.
She sighs
in infinite sadness and despair
as she bears her burden
alone.

A Dream

I had a dream.
Two small girls were
in a bedroom in the house
next door to Grandma's.
They screamed
   and screamed
and I was terrified,
standing on the porch next door.
My sister came
and told me to forget what I had heard
for there was nothing we could do
to help.

I have come to wonder
what the dream might mean
and if the little girls
were really we.

Third-Grade Teacher

Dear Third-Grade Teacher:

You found me daydreaming today.
Usually I work real hard
   finish on time
   read lots of books
   write poems that rhyme
and act like a very good girl.
You scolded me
again
because I was dreaming.

You didn't know that
yesterday
when no one else was home
Daddy made me lie on the couch
with all my clothes off.
He just sat in his big chair
and looked at me
smiling a smile I can't understand.
I was ashamed
embarrassed and afraid.

Today I couldn't remember
my "times eights"
and I spent the April afternoon
daydreaming.
You didn't understand.

Dying

Sometimes I wished I would be
a happily-ever-after princess
or that I would die.
It bothered me that if I died
you might not care (Mother would).
Faced with dying
I preferred to put the living thoughts
and memories away
deep in my head
where no one could see—
not even me.
I died
inside.

Uncle Louie

Uncle Louie always gave little girls
a big kiss.
Everybody smiled.
It was a French kiss
and I wondered why it was
so wet
and what a little girl should do.
I looked to Mommy and Daddy and Aunt Bernice.
They hadn't noticed—
    or so it seemed.
I suppose they wouldn't dare believe
    that anything was wrong.
They looked over my head
and smiled at Uncle Louie.
I guess it's okay, I thought.
Maybe every little girl
should like her uncle's kiss.
I looked at Uncle Louie
and I smiled too.

Music

When I was young
I knew a lot of torch songs—
   blues.
People thought it odd
that someone only ten or twelve
should like such songs
and sing them with such feeling.

ADOLESCENT

Survival

Eyes can be blank.
They can refuse to see
whatever body or person
is thrust before them.
If you squeeze your eyes tight
and hold them shut
until they hurt
and think to yourself
  this is not happening
  I'll pretend I'm not here
  I won't think about it
over and over and over
you can forget
in order to survive.

Twelve

One terrible night
you asked too much.
I was twelve—
far too small and young
to resist.
My tears burned my eyes
and my throat filled with lead
which I swallowed
until I turned into a statue—
a metal sculpture.
I would never
be warm again.

Sex Education

Sex education.

I was quite surprised
by all the facts and advice
I learned in that movie.
Mom had been pretty shy
about telling me
although she tried.
So I watched and listened
every year when they showed
that movie to the girls.

When I was thirteen
I took special note
of when a girl's body can conceive—
in case I needed to know . . .

I needed to know.

Thirteen

Textbooks say that thirteen
is the age when one
wrestles with identity.
Am I weak or strong
    loved or rejected
    female or male
    capable or inept?
Who am I? the child-adult wonders.
I wondered too.

I stood before the screen door
looking at the countryside
from Grandpa's house in summer.
I was blank inside
    lonely
    bored
    wondering.
I was struggling
    wrestling
not just with identity
    but with what you said about me
    by what you did.
I was weak—
    you always won.
I was rejected—
    you went away angry.
I was female—
    and hated it.
I was not capable
    because I could not change my life.

Young, tender, frightened
I was a textbook case of the struggle
and doomed to lose.
A blank empty life
    looking out the screen door.

Junior High

Embarrassed.
I was humiliated
when you handled me
in front of your friends.
Mocked
because they talked about
how I was becoming a woman
and they laughed.
You were the leader of the pack.
The wolves
devoured my self-esteem
leaving me bleeding
to face the kids at school
who didn't know
why I was so timid—
    friendly
    but afraid of boys.

I look back on those days
as the worst of all.
Days when humiliation
spoiled every success,
and pride
was abandoned in the bloody snow
to cold cruel wolves.

Eighth Grade

It was the one time I fought.
I first refused your invitation.
I kept playing my piano lesson.
  I played on
  you spoke
  I refused and played on.
Then you spoke again.
No, I said.
I don't want to do that anymore.
I didn't look at you.
I kept my fingers on the keys.
You grabbed me:
  "Come here, I said!"
I wasn't strong enough.
I pulled away
  but the wood hall floor
  was slippery.
I lost.
I lost it all.
I was young, fourteen.
I never fought again.

Other Dads

My friends had nice dads—
men who talked to us
from their easy chairs
where they read the paper
when we came to visit.
My girlfriends would wave good-bye
or give their dads a kiss
as they left for the show
or to go skating.
I never understood it.
And I seldom asked girlfriends over
when you were home.
I wasn't sure I dared.

Posture

I'm one of the round-shouldered women.
People tend to think
it's because I'm tall.
Perhaps.
More likely it's because
when I was fifteen
you teased me about my breasts,
my budding womanhood.
You used gutter words.
My chest has been sunken in
since then.
The irony is you used to tell me
   "Stand straight
   Shoulders back
   Walk proud."

Sixteen

When I was sixteen
we lived by a lake.
All the kids went swimming
at the beach every day.
I heard they had a great time
  swimming
  sunning
  teasing.
I stayed home.
I couldn't tell anyone my reasons.
I was embarrassed
  to show myself
  in a scant suit
and ashamed to be a woman.
My femininity already spoiled,
sixteen wasn't sweet.

Adolescence

Most adolescents resist
parental coddling or direction.
Part of growing up
is getting angry
   disappointed
   and disgusted with parents.
All my friends did it.
I'd complain too
   when Mom was overcautious
   or grouchy.

I hardly said a word about you.
I seethed in quiet.
I pretended all was well
and they seldom saw you.
But it didn't change my attitude.
I hated you.

You and i

You
Are
A
Selfish
Terrifying
Cruel
Person
  and
  i
  can't
  find
  anyplace
  to
  hide.

Fickle

I'd date boys at college.
If I liked one too much
I got scared.
When I liked someone deeply
I was afraid to feel.
Touching and loving
was so compelling,
   so desirable.
Suddenly a mist of change
would envelop me.
I'd hate the boy
   look for faults
   draw away.
We'd part
and I'd feel guilty
because I'd been unfair.
Fickle youthful years.

It has taken nearly twenty more
to understand.
I didn't hate the boys at all.
I was only afraid
to love them.
Afraid they'd hurt me,
treat me nicely
just to get some favors,
draw away or scold me—
leave.
Just like you.

WOMAN

Nightmares

I lived in the shadow of dreams,
frightening nightmares
that would cause me to awaken,
silent screams tearing through my mind.
I pleaded with the darkness
to take away my fears.
But the dreams returned
   often unexpectedly
   sometimes vague
   sometimes repetitious.
I could not run away.

Struggle

I'm afraid of dying.
More afraid than many
    because I know it's real.
It's me who dies—
    I can't deny it
    as others do.
I've seen death
    in his menacing eyes
    a too-sharp grabbing of my arm
    a blow to my young cheek
and in a vivid sense of being marked
    Unwanted.
I've known the brink
    of the power of death
    over which I had no control.

I struggle now
    against an abiding deep force
that would destroy
    not only my body
    but my inner soul—
destroy my concept of my Self
    my will to survive
    my joy of life.
Every day I fight to live.

Vocation

Once I thought
my goal in life
could be to make men happy.
Men—
not a man.
It occurred to me
that a prostitute has a good purpose.
She pleases men.
It scares me to think
I might have tried it.
It seemed to fit.

Secrets

To love a man in secret
has always seemed
   more exciting
   high-charged
   and wonderful.
When I was very small
that's how it seemed to me—
a wonderful secret!

Now I struggle to reconcile
my past and my present,
and a recurring desire
for meaningless secret love.

A Patsy

I used to say to friends
I'm a patsy
  for compliments
  or special gifts
  or kindness
from a man.
Not only that I was pleased
or felt cared for
when a man treated me that way.
But that I hoped I was loved,
and in feeling so glad
I might do anything he wanted
just to please him.
A patsy.

Aloof

A man told me
I was aloof.
No doubt I was—
    stiff gestures
    demure presence
    cautious smiles
    and serious.
I had to keep my defenses up
especially around him.
He couldn't know
why I needed affectations
of distance
in order to feel safe
around men
especially those I liked.

Princess

I fell in love
with a young man
who called me Princess.
I always thought
it was a nice endearment
and a pleasant dream—
something a father
might call his little girl.

But the young man left too.

Older Men

Older men often seem nice.
Especially men like my grandpa.
They seem to want to take care of me
   gently tease
   protect me.
I feel close to them.
I need their attention.

One man
   (or was it many, in my dreams)
was slightly younger than my father.
He loved me
   I could tell
and I so dearly wanted to be his.
It could have been a repetition
of my past
with a chance for a happy ending.
Maybe this time
my lover-father
   wouldn't hurt me
   would hold me close
   and stay.

I couldn't take the risk.
I sent him away.

Legacy

I began to realize
I could hurt my children.
I might teach them
   to abuse
   to use
   to take advantage
of others, of sexuality.
Or I might keep them
stained
   in some subtle way
by my past.
That was when I knew
I must discover
   what was wrong with me.
I must try to change.
I must go for help.

THERAPY

Therapist

Help me, I pleaded—
never saying the words
but crying out in frightened eyes
   legs clasped tight together
   or drawn up to my chest
   arms stiff
   body hunched.
You were skilled enough
to know the signs
and kind enough to wait
with gentle encouragement
until I could trust you
   and tell.

Telling you
was the beginning of my life.
You heard my plea
and understood.

Acute Memory

My friends tell me
they don't remember anything that happened
when they were small.
That's because we don't need to remember
   most experiences
   word for word.

One who must protect oneself—
   be on guard
   measure sincerity
   beware of harm
dares not forget the good
and especially the bad.

I remember being three.
Somewhere underneath my thinking
my childhood stays with me.

Self-Hate

What I cannot bear
is knowing that I wanted you—
not in spirit
   only body.
I hate that predictable response
of a young woman
   to a demanding
   skillful man.
I hate that reality
because it was me.
I cannot forgive.
I live
   the intolerable misery
of hating not only you
but me.

Grief

Sometimes a record does it.
The music touches
a deep emptiness in me.
I acknowledge that I've never known
the love of a father.
Less an orphan
more an abandoned baby
I am a chipped vessel
from which the water of spirit flows,
diminishing me.
Empty,
I am left only tears
until the grief passes.

Counseling

I need to be held.
Someone to hold me
  rock me
  nurture me
in a safe place
where I can trust
and not be used.
I come again to one
who understands my need
and respects my body
and my soul.
I am held
with integrity and caring.
I learn
that it is possible
to be loved.

Recollection

I awakened this morning uneasy—
unable or afraid to recall a dream.
I went about my day
but I knew he had returned.

Was I eight
   or seventeen?
I wasn't sure.
I only knew
from the wavering feeling
   in my stomach
   and my hands
there was more to recollect.
Another dismal
   or frightening moment
was ready to unfold.

I took a breath
and called for an appointment.
I would face it soon in therapy
and put it behind me.
My sigh reveals
I tire of the need
to face the truth
   again
   and again.

Escape

Take it away!
Take away the truth.
Let me pretend
I was like all my girlfriends.
I had a normal, loving life.
I was a happy child.
Let me forget the past
   the truth.

Shame

I don't like to remember
because, like everyone else,
I'm ashamed to know.
Each memory
lowers my head
 nearly to my chest
in shame.
I feel worthless, ugly.
I beg of myself
reasons why I didn't resist.
Even when I know that I was helpless
 and unable to stop
 the gradual debasement of my soul
I long to believe I didn't succumb.

Point of View

A grown woman
realizes what she did for years
to appease
   and please her father.
Even though she's been told
   and knows in her mind
that she had no choice
from early childhood on,
she feels responsible
   somehow at fault
   or perhaps deserving.
Weak, disgraced, ashamed
her only hope is that
once she realizes and weeps,
she can start to recognize
it wasn't she who failed at all.
She is the victim
not the criminal.

Family

Where were you when I needed you?
What you didn't know
    you might have guessed.
But you chose to overlook
because to see was painful.
I bore your pain
    plus all of mine
while you ignored me.
Where the hell were you?

Cause and Effect

Somewhere inside you
there must be a chasm—
   an ache
   rejection
   abuse
a feeling of being inadequate.
Your empty hollow waited
probably for years—
   twenty, twenty-seven,
until I came.

Then, rather than relieving
   your ache
by welcoming my life—
   a new start
   a baby
   a joy
you chose to take away my Self,
cruelly stuff my hope
   into your septic hollow—
   rejection
   abuse
   contamination.

I am left with your burden
and my despair.

Thirty-six

It took me more than
thirty-six years
to say aloud that
you were cruel
   thoughtless
   selfish
   using me.
Even then I fairly whispered
   the words.
I was still protecting you.
Now my stomach turns and slides
as I find myself
   still making excuses
   denying truth
   turning anger in on myself
as I cover up your weakness.
I am destroying me
by protecting you.
I've done it for thirty-six years.

Maturity

I'm always a little afraid
I'll lose control.
I'll perpetuate the destructive chain
    if not in my family
    then among acquaintances
or that I'll regress to my old ways.
I feel fear creep through my body
shaking each nerve in succession
overpowering me
    as you once did.
I beg to be strong enough
    to stand firm
    unafraid
    trusting me.
I long to feel free.

Exploitation

People easily take advantage of me.
When I was young
it was often young men
   charming
   handsome
or especially appealing people
   who seemed to need me—
it was they who took advantage
of my patience or affections.
Now it is others—
   husband, children
   relatives
   pastors, leaders
   and especially friends
   who are in trouble, needing me.

I know it isn't only they
   who are at fault.
While they accept my offerings
of time, money
   kindness, patience
   and my reluctance to confront
it is I who allow the exploitation.
I haven't learned how to say no.
It is a habit I developed
in exploitive relationship
   with you.

My Body

I don't really dare
have a body.
I try not to think about it
or picture how it looks.
I don't really appreciate it
care for it in tender ways.
I hide my body
in nonseductive clothes
or sloping shoulders,
proper behavior
and in my reluctance
to go to a public beach.
Don't look!
Please, don't see.
This body belongs to me
and I'm afraid to show it
because I'm afraid to lose it.
It doesn't help much
to say that I look nice.
I'm ashamed
of what this body has done
and afraid to have it happen again.
I'm holding on to myself.
No one will have me
unless I let them.
I've lost too many times before.
I'm afraid to have a body.

Bitterness

I'm not bitter.
Mother loved me,
though she lacked the courage
to protect me
and resist you.
She lives inside me
and helps to cancel bitterness.
I'm not bitter.

But I hate.
I hate that weakness in you
that knowingly destroyed
my childlike wonder
and soured my life for years.
I hate you.

Techniques

There are books
full of diagrams, drawings
and techniques for lovemaking.
Since I've been married
I've read them,
trying to understand
why I was so unwilling
to give myself.
Only after getting help
have I understood
that the diagrams
stirred up old feelings
and ugly memories.
I knew the techniques
long before I wanted to know.

Fantasy

I have called a meeting.
Everyone in my family has come.
Anticipation brightens the air—
    an announcement
    good news may be coming.

Then I begin the story:
A father and an unsuspecting daughter.
I don't even need all the details.
By their silence I know they understand
(perhaps they already knew, without my
speaking).
I enjoy their shock
    and shame
    and disgust.
I am glad they can't get away.
They can't leave me
    holding the ugly truth anymore.

And you.
You sit wooden
but your flesh peels away
with the sweat rising on your brow.
You cannot run
    too weak to resist.
I have my revenge.
You are exposed!

A fantasy.

Crazy

This is crazy.
I am crying
   screaming
   hiding my face in shame.
I am weak
and can't rest.
My stomach is like a stone and
my fingers ache from clenching.
I suffer.

You!
You walk calmly
among people, relatives.
They don't know you
as I do.
You smile
and feel no guilt
   no shame.
You walk away from my pain.

This is crazy.
I carry the weight of the sentence
but you are the killer.

Confessions

After therapy
I was afraid to tell
any of my friends
   especially men.
I was ashamed
afraid they might abandon me.
Gradually I tested them.
I told my story.
After they had taken time
to comprehend the truth
they comforted
they cared—
another proof that
   there is Good
   past is gone.
I am not spoiled
   a ruined, lessened person.
They care for me.

Hate

Hate
Hate
Hate
Hate
Hate
Hate
Hate
Hate
Hate
Hate
Hate
Hate
Why me?

Relief

At times during therapy
I'm afraid I'll be sick someday—
physically sick
if I have to remember.
But just before I leave
for the counselor's office
I often have a surge of strength.
I'm ready.
I've never become ill
when I faced the truth—
 only relieved.

Volcano

God! Take away this awful time!
I can't hold my hatred in
and I'm afraid to let it fly.
If I let it go
    outside a safe environment
it may hurt someone innocent.
God, give me a safe place
    a safe person
who can help me *be*
without destroying someone else
or me.

Anger

Anger
was never allowed.
No matter what you did or I felt
I was not to say my anger—
and in time not even to feel it.
A petrified egg
    smooth, hard
    and full of mystery.
I would have thrown all the eggs!
all the lies! the names!
all the unfairness in your face
in my anger
rage!
But I was not allowed.
I could only push it down inside.

Years later, I felt a change.
I had begun to hear other people's anger
and admit it could be mine.
I saw my fists clench more often
    my neck tense
    my stomach . . .
My stomach began to ache, pain
at the mention of you.
And anger—
I knew it was time to find a way
to set it free.
My body was ready to release the rage
whatever form it might take.
I could contain it no more.

My task was to find a way
to be me—
to be honestly furious
hurting no one
but setting me free.
I would find a way.

I who would never write on walls
found a photo of you, full-length
and had it made nearly life-size.
I took it with me
and alongside in a shopping bag
artifacts
    cigars
    unwanted gifts
    poker chips
    a father's day card
memories and symbols of you.
And I brought weapons
    a knife
    razor blade
    and powerful words
    saved for nearly a lifetime.

I carefully thought it through
    fists clenched and stomach tight.
I went to the place where I was safe
guarded by the strength and understanding
of the counselor who knew.

There I began to say the truth,
   first to my listener and me
   then to my aggressor, the photograph.
I needed a place to begin
and when I said "It was wrong!"
I knew I would not stop until I finished.
I spoke the words and spat the anger!
Bitterness, disgust
   and a growing realization
   it was no longer I who was "wrong."
I did not deserve to have been hurt!
Rage!
Powerful, real, honest, explosive rage
saved for years and years—
   finally set free.

I knew it was safe to say and feel.
No one would be hurt.
On my knees before a photograph
I became taller—
tall enough to be real
tall enough to be free.

I was no longer captive to threat
   or memories
   or self-hate.
I gave the hate its proper place
and stood up
a new person.

I would never write on walls.
But photographs and father's day cards
even newsprint and broken ashtrays
carried my words.
Strewn about a private room
were the symbols of the release
of a little girl.
When she was able to say "I hate"
she was able to say
   "but I don't hate me"
and in that moment perhaps begin
a slow, patient walk toward forgiveness
or at least acceptance.

A grown-up little girl
set free.

HEALING

Decision

Now that I remember,
have worked through my past
and how it lives in me today,
I can make a choice.
I can talk with you Dad
   tell you how I feel
and prepare myself
   for all the ways you may respond
   (I'll practice them).
Or I can leave you
far behind
walk away
   and start again
create a separate life
where only memories can reach me.
You cannot touch me there.

Either choice is difficult.
I must wait
to see what's best to do—
   best not for you
   but best for *me*.

Behavior Modification

When my husband touches me
I have to tell my mind
   my stomach
   my eyes
   my skin
it is my husband
   it is not you.
It is all right now.
It is good to be loved
   and wanted—
   to give ungrudgingly.
I have to tell myself
over and over
and sometimes I relax
and love is good.

Watercolors

It was a watercolor painting—
bright yellow discovery
set jauntily beside sweet orange innocence.
With quiet strokes
came green familiarity
and a blue promise of love.
Then unexpectedly a streak
of black awareness—
    innocence spoiled.
Red spilled across the paper—
passion on the edge
of purple fear.
Colors running together
until there was nothing left pure—
    not innocence
    not tenderness
    not even the joy of genuine passion.
Only a gray portrait
of the confusion and destruction
of a child become woman.

Victim

I think I'm fine
and life is going well.
Then one day when I'm tired
someone disagrees with me
and I'm frantic
   as if their disagreement
   is urgent
   threatening
   must be overcome.
I struggle with them
   internally, externally
mustering words like troops
ready to fight.

Often it takes days
before I realize
there was no battle to win.
I had only slipped backwards
feeling as when a child
struggling with you.
Since I had no power then
I desperately gather power now.
I learned so young
what it is to be victim
I hardly know how to believe
I can win—
and I lose again.

Children

I know now
I shall always be afraid
for children.
I watch them
   and adults nearby
wary, cautious
ready to protect the helpless
if they need me.
It's a magnified reaction
which may never change
because it is reality for me
based on my experience
with you.

Remembering Youth

We were talking together
about what it means to be an adolescent—
the pains of growing
and of meeting people's expectations.
We were parents
and we had almost forgotten
how trying it is to grow up.
To help us recall, we closed our eyes
and tried to remember our teenage days—
    where we had lived
    what school we attended
    who were our friends
    what did we wear.
I closed my eyes with the others
and I saw the house
    the school
    my friend
    and . . . him.
HIM!
watching me
touching me
wanting me to do things
I didn't want to do.
All the adolescent feelings returned—
    fear, embarrassment, shame
    rage, shame, worthlessness, guilt
    shame.

My eyes filled with tears
and I left the room to cry.
I remember the years too well.
Perhaps I will understand
better than some mothers
what it means to feel the pain
of adolescence.
Perhaps I will know
more than I care to remember.

Powerful Words

Everybody has a word or two
that carries extra power.
For some they are four-letter words
    coarse
    dramatic
or attacks on religion.
No-no words
    that call up
    shocks of the heart
    imbalance of senses
    ugly thoughts.
Everyone has some of those words.

I was amazed to learn from friends
that two of my powerful words
are not shocking
    or blasphemous
    to them
    or to most people.
All these years
    my heart pounded
    and my mind worried
    whenever I heard them said.
I wouldn't say them aloud.
My words were
    touch
    and kiss.

Well-meaning

There have been those
I sought to have help me—
some trained in religious conviction
some friends who wanted to help.
They meant well.
But neither they
    nor I
knew how deep this problem was
nor how to handle it.
Generally after a short while
I could tell
I wasn't being helped at all.
I was being judged
    or questioned
    or misunderstood.
I needed more.
They meant well
but sometimes I took a backwards step
in seeking them.
It is important to know
what one is unable to do.
I wish they had told me
to turn to someone else
    a professional
    who knew.
Perhaps we all have learned
something about the limits
of those who want to help.
Next time I hope they'll refer.

Spring Afternoon

Driving down the street on a spring afternoon
I saw an old man on the sidewalk,
bent posture and wavering walk.
Well-dressed, he steadied himself on his car
and cautiously began to step toward the street.
He was too old to drive, I thought,
a plucky fellow, perhaps eighty years.
I felt sorry for him.

As my car approached and he turned to
walk to the door of his,
I realized he was no stranger—
he was my father.
Tears!
Stinging tears.
We hadn't spoken for three years.
My deep desire to stop, to say hello
and my rage of hate and anger
ran together across my eyes and cheeks.
I speeded up my car, pulled down the sunshade
and watched from the sideview mirror
as he entered his car.
An old man, powerless though only sixty-five,
he seemed eighty.

Beat my hands into the couch!
Cry aloud
that life has given me such confusion
love and pity mixed with hate and fear.
No simple answer and no return—
no way out.
He can no longer hurt me
yet the burden of the load of
painful memories and unresolved confusion
destroys the beauty of a spring afternoon
and my compassion for an old man.

Fear

Fear is still a way of life.
Afraid of closets
being in a boat on a lake
or alone in an elevator
of dark streets
anger
hunting trophies
men
attics
my body
blocked doorways
men
shotguns
loud reveling.

Fear of never being able
to let someone love me.

God

I've been glad for God the Spirit
and for God the Son
because I don't believe
my heart can ever understand
that God is like a father.

Forgiveness

There are those who expect me to forgive
to let charitable kindness and reason
wash over me
    like a rushing stream
    over jagged rocks—
to forgive
now.

Seventy times seven—
the command may mean more
than first appears.
Not that one says "I forgive"
over and over and over
nor that to will it
    makes it so,
but that one forgives
    as one loves—
gradually.
Forgiveness is a process
that begins with knowledge
    understanding
    believing in change.
I feel little charity now.
I can hope
    it may happen
    as I come to understand
    myself and you.
Seventy experiences and understandings
    times seven or seventy more.
I can believe I will forgive
    someday—then.

Courage

A friend told me
that my past was not important—
what matters is that I had
the courage to face it.
Courage!
Me?
After all the years of hiding
and repressing the truth
in fear
I am now the one
called brave!
I'm proud.

Change

On a quiet September night
barely warm from summer
I breathe the world—
fresh, renewing.
A deep breath.
At last relaxed.
My body is able now
   to cry
   to touch
   to play—
even, now and then, to trust.
My body breathes freely
because it belongs at last
to me.

Redemption

I am now able
to help someone else—
   listen to her stories
   tell her that I love her
   promise it will get better
   and say how brave she is
   and strong!
I can say I understand
and share her anger,
and sometimes gently touch
her frightened face
and say it is all right.
I can tell her she is beautiful
even when she feels debased.
And now and then
she lets me hold her,
lets me share her deepest pain
the loneliness of her mistrust.
I am healed enough
to help someone else
and find that all my pain
has greater meaning.
In sharing love
my trauma is redeemed.